AF492927

HEARTWARMING ANIMAL PALS STORIES FOR KIDS OF ALL AGES

By Robert F. Burgess

308 W. Marion Street
Chattahoochee, Florida 32324

HEARTWARMING ANIMAL PALS STORIES FOR KIDS OF ALL AGES

By Robert F. Burgess

Dedicated to animal lovers everywhere
Especially those caregivers in
Animal sanctuaries throughout the world

TABLE OF CONTENTS

CHAPTER 1

The Dog Who Loved an Elephant

When I was a young boy my Grandpa told me that nobody knew where elephants went to die because their graveyard had never been found, I never forgot it. He said that whoever found it would be rich beyond their wildest dreams because the place would be filled with very valuable ivory tusks.

Wow, I thought, what if a person found a place like that! I knew, from my Mom and Dad that dogs often went off by themselves when they were sick or about to die. When Smoky my pet cat disappeared I was told that cats were very independent. If they got it in their heads that they had had enough of being a pet they often just went off to take up the life of a roving vagabond, just like pirates. That didn't sound too bad to me. My missing cat didn't die after all because all cats had nine lives and he was probably just off enjoying one of those lives filled with lots of exploration and adventure.

As I grew older the tale of the elephant graveyard that no one had ever found continued to intrigue me. To my mind that mysterious hidden graveyard full of tusks had to be somewhere in Africa where I thought all elephants lived. Maybe when they knew they were going to die they went to a hidden cave that one day someone would find and it would be filled with centuries of extremely valuable ivory tusks. What an adventure that would be, to go to Africa and search for that long lost elephant graveyard! Elephants were such big animals I wondered why nobody had ever followed an old one to see where he went when it was his time to go.

When I grew up I became a writer of true adventure books. The new world of exploration and adventure that was just opening for my generation was the underwater world. The closest I ever got to that African elephant graveyard mystery was to interview early scuba divers who had done a near impossible thing. They had dived down to over 190 feet in a giant underwater cavern in Florida to explore it and discovered a cathedral sized bone-yard of prehistoric elephant ancestors called mastodons!

WOW! There it was! At least for our elephant ancestors. As a young author I quickly wrote about it in a book titled *The Cave Divers*; and later as an e-book titled, *Mastodon at Thirty-three Fathoms*.

Those early cave-diving explorers had made an incredible discovery in northwest Florida's Wakulla Spring. They ended up recovering an entire mastodon skeleton for the state museum in Tallahassee. No wonder no one found it! This elephant ancestor's secret cavern was probably dry when our elephant ancestors had gone there during the Ice Age when seas were 300 feet lower. Or perhaps they had fallen into this death trap when it was a spring. We will never know. But in my mind the real secret elephant place where old elephants went to die was still in "Darkest Africa"…or was it all just a tantalizing tale that never died?

What made that tale live forever were all those valuable ivory tusks. Like all lost treasure stories they tantalize generations of wannabe treasure hunters until one of them finally finds the treasure, or learns the truth…that it was just a tale for the ages. Like the Lost Dutchman mine in Arizona's Superstition Mountains or the Oak Island buried treasure currently being mined by a television series.

Interestingly, elephant experts today believe that rather than African elephants, the prehistoric mastodons were closer in ancestral linage to our Asian elephants, the species this story is about. Still, my Grandpa's story always charmed me.

Then one day I learned that there was an important place where old elephants went to enjoy their final days right here in our own US of A!

Called the Elephant Sanctuary located just south of Nashville, Tennessee, over 2,000 acres of natural woodlands and grasslands are especially set aside for elderly elephants where they can live out their lives in quiet comfort without being bothered by us spectators, known collectively as "the public."

Many of these rescued elephants were old circus performers, or had lived in zoos, or had otherwise fallen on hard times. Today, ten of these Asian elephants are allowed to roam free in this Green Eden while all their needs are taken care of by concerned caregivers.

All of which provides me with a reason to tell you about a most unusual bond of friendship between Tarra, a sanctuary elephant, and a stray dog named Bella.

Tarra is famous as the only 8,000-pound roller-skating lady elephant in the world. She once performed in the movie *Annie*, and appeared in the television series, "Little House on the Prairie." She was the first elephant to enter the Green Eden of this Tennessee Elephant Sanctuary, but other elephants soon followed. Tarra the circus elephant met each new arrival and took it upon herself to show them around. She took them from the elephant barn across the pastures, showed them her favorite horse trails and the lakes where they could swim and bathe; she seemed pleased to be able to do this. She even showed them how she picked huckleberries with her trunk.

As more new elephants came, they usually developed special friendships with other elephants. But not Tarra, who often flirted with dogs as though she wanted a dog friend; but she never bonded in close friendship with any of the other elephants. And not too oddly, the dogs she flirted with had no intention of getting very close to this large lady with the big feet.

The caring person who started the Elephant Sanctuary in

Tennessee was Carol Buckley. Carol and Tarra were old friends. The two had been together for years because they both were long-time professional circus performers. Carol was a pretty, trim-figured performer who knew what delight and awe she and her friend brought to audiences. The two of them made a stunning couple together. The small pretty woman in her silver and black sequined costume riding atop the massive gray head and large ears of such a humongously huge elephant was a sight to behold.

How it must have startled the circus crowds when the tall curtains parted and with a fanfare of trumpets from the circus band, accompanied by a long increasingly louder roll of snare drums ending in a crash of cymbals, the spotlight swung across and glaringly lighted them as the two entered the ring.

With their hearts pounding thanks to the dramatic buildup, the crowds stared in disbelief. Smiling and waving to the stunned stands of screaming children and awed parents, the pretty lady astride her giant gray steed paused in this glaring light letting the crowds savor the sight. Then with light pressure of her knees the lady signaled Tarra and the two stepped forward into the ring. The band struck up a rousing number and the showman with the loudspeaker told the crowds what spellbinding things they were about to see.

Both Carol and Tarra loved this hoopla. They had enjoyed it together for years. Exciting performances were why everyone liked going to the circus. No matter how many times they did it, it was always exciting to these professional performers. They loved the brassy music that always announced them; then the noisy clamor and the clapping hands that always greeted her and her talented friend, Tarra. Those moments when the two of them performed amazing things for their enraptured audiences were magical moments that they would never forget.

But after 20 years of performing with her elephant, Carol knew it was time to let Tarra retire so that she could enjoy her old age without having to perform any more.

Carol bought Tarra from the circus and eventually, along with her friend Scott Blais, the two former animal trainers accomplished the long-held dream they both wanted. In 1995 they purchased the extensive wild acreage south of Nashville near Hohenwald, Tennessee where the two of them opened the Elephant Sanctuary, a haven that offered a refuge for all stray and abused dogs as well. The public was not to be allowed into this sanctuary because it was intended just for the animals that would live there in a semi-tropical zone where all their needs would now be the responsibility of the sanctuary's caregivers.

This sanctuary is in rolling country with lots of trees and grassy meadows. The property also includes a lake. The animal residents have the freedom to roam and enjoy these natural surroundings without any interference while they are tenderly cared for. The elephants quietly enjoy the natural countryside while relating to one another during the time they have together.

For Carol and Scott it was the dream of their lives and Tarra was the first retired elephant actress to enjoy it. Soon, other elephants arrived to join her. At first it was a strange new world to these older performers who had never before had such wonderful freedom in such a lush environment. Sometimes it took a while for them to realize how fortunate they were.

The caregivers knew the names of all their elephants and were dedicated to making their lives just as comfortable as possible. Each new elephant arrival was always greeted by the other elephants who welcomed them into their herd. This particular trait is common to all elephants and those who study such things are constantly amazed at how warm and loving these gentle giants are to each other.

Before long many of the elephants paired up with other elephants and developed special friendships with them. These pairs always looked forward to sharing their days together, whether it was just roaming the countryside or enjoying meals together. The bonds they made lasted a lifetime.

Carol noticed that for some reason Tarra never seemed interested in bonding with any of the other elephants. She was often alone and Carol worried that she might lose interest in life if she didn't develop a bond with one of the other members of the herd. But Tarra apparently felt no need for that. The herd soon numbered ten adult female elephants. Tarra joined them for walks and other activities, but she often spent time alone, simply standing and pondering whatever solitary elephants ponder when they are satisfied with things.

Since rescued dogs were also welcomed at the sanctuary many became permanent residents. They kept out of the way of the elephants that were not too happy with their constant barking and running around underfoot. Consequently, the dogs and the elephants usually gave each other lots of room.

Carol was always on the lookout for abandoned dogs in need of a home. Driving back and forth along the gravel road to the sanctuary she often saw a small cream-colored dog at an abandoned farm near the sanctuary. It hung around a rusty yellow bulldozer parked behind the farm in the weed-choked backyard.

A couple times Carol had pulled into the place trying to make friends with the dog but she failed. Carol saw that the young dog had no collar and seemed afraid of people. She talked soothingly to the stray, but the dog always bared her teeth, growled and ran off to hide under the bulldozer. Carol wondered how in the world she kept herself alive in this deserted place. She thought probably by drinking rainwater and finding field mice in the overgrown fields behind the dozer. So sad.

Repeatedly, Carol tried to befriend the orphan with the appealing brown eyes and wide smile, but the dog always avoided her. She always showed her teeth, accompanied by a low throaty growl, to let all intruders know that she might be a young pup, but she would put up with no nonsense from strangers.

Finally, one bitterly cold winter's day as she drove along that gravel road, Carol again glimpsed the dog sitting beside the bulldozer, so once more she turned in at the farm.

As she got out of her truck, the dog took one look at her and ducked into a shallow hole she had dug under the dozer.

Carol approached the machine slowly, talking quietly to the frightened dog. But this time instead of showing her teeth the dog looked up at her from her hole and growled. Carol knew it was not a menacing growl. The look in those soft brown eyes told Carol that she was just afraid. Her eyes were wide with fear and she was trembling.

As Carol got down on the ground and kept talking soothingly to the frightened dog she heard the growl turn to whimpering whines. Carol saw that the dog wanted to come out to her but she was so afraid. Carol took off her glove and slowly extended her warm hand. The dog sniffed it suspiciously. Still whining quietly she let the woman touch her. Carol's warm hand slowly stroked the dog's thin trembling side.

Finally, the pup gave in to her soft words and soft touches. Ducking her head and with her tail tightly drawn up under her, the pup pawed at the earth in an effort to move herself out of her hole. Emboldened by what she saw, Carol carefully reached down and drew her out.

The young circus performer who had worked with circus animals all of her life cradled the cream-colored little dog in her arms and hugged her. She felt the trembling as the little dog leaned in close to her warm breast and looked up at her face with such sad eyes that Carol wanted to cry.

She didn't know if the people who had lived at the farm abandoned the dog when they left, or why the dog was guarding the big yellow machine. Maybe she was waiting for the return of its long departed owner, her master. Either way it was obvious that no one was coming back to claim this abandoned little orphan. Carol smiled down at the sad-eyed youngster and knew exactly where her new home would be.

Cradling her in her arms, Carol continued to talk softly and reassuringly to the pup as she made a warm place for her in a cardboard box with a thin red blanket she always carried in the truck for animals in distress. She put the box on the passenger side of her front seat where the heater would warm the dog. Then she deposited the whimpering pup and tucked her in with the blanket.

Back on the road again, smiling happily to herself as the new part-owner of the brand new elephant sanctuary headed there with one very lucky little dog, Carol already had a name for her. Her name would be Bella, because that's what she was – beautiful.

The little rescued dog named Bella grew up in a wonderful new world from that she had been enduring. She easily made friends with people and the other stray dogs that lived at the sanctuary.

As time passed Carol and Bella became close friends. What was so amazing, however, was how the little cream-colored bundle of energy responded to her first tour of the sanctuary with Carol in her blue truck. Bella the dog was so startled to see elephants that for the first time in her life she forgot to bark. She just stared, wide-eyed and silent as they drove past these huge gray animals. She was fascinated by the lumbering shapes that reminded her so much of the one she had guarded so long waiting for her master to return. The difference was that these animals were alive and moved. They were the most exciting things this little cream-colored dog could even imagine.

After the truck ride through the sanctuary Carol and her stray dog friend walked the grassy acres every morning and then for the first time ever, Bella and Tarra saw each other.

There was no stopping Bella, with a joyful yip she bounded off and raced circles around the dumbfounded Tarra, not barking wildly like some of the stray dogs but whining in excitement.

Tarra too responded excitedly, sort of chirping and

making an "Ummmm," sound deep in her throat the way elephants often do when they enjoy the meal they are eating. Carol was delighted that the two of them hit it off so well. Carol had long thought that Tarra was destined to be lonely because she had not committed herself to bond closely with any of the other elephants there. Carol realized for years that this quiet, almost painfully shy, big elephant had a special liking for dogs. Carol had noticed how the elephant seemed especially attracted to the little furry creatures, but none of the dogs she met ever returned any of that friendship she so wanted to have with them.

But now, the first time Tarra and Bella met, it was like magic. Both of them seemed determined to become close friends. Carol couldn't have been more pleased.

From then on the dog and the elephant were inseparable. They took long walks together exploring the sanctuary, they ate together and they slept in the same barn together. To watch the two of them together no one would doubt but that they were extremely fond of each other.

The sanctuary had a lake that the elephants all enjoyed. Tarra and Bella got in the water and frolicked together, the large lumbering Tarra not able to match Bella's swift moves but her eyes danced as she saw how excited Bella was swimming around her. She even climbed atop the elephant's large rounded back that Tarra purposely lowered enough so that her dog-paddling companion could clamor aboard, barking excitedly as she did. The two of them acted more like excited children playing in the water together. If Bella was riding on Tarra's back, the elephant would suck up a trunk-full (2½ gallons) of water and spray it all over the barking Bella. If she did that twice, that was enough for Bella and she would do a belly-flop back into the water.

Once the two frisky bathers climbed out of the lake, if there was loose dirt nearby Tarra gave herself a dirt shower with her handy trunk. With water on her back the dirt quickly turned to mud. Tarra did this not because she liked to get dirty but because once the mud dried it provided her with a caked on coat of protection from sunburn and biting insects. From dry sand beside the lake she treated herself to a trunk blown sand bath. She knew that some would stick and protect her. But she also knew how to play a trick on Bella with sand that did not stick to her back.

Whenever Bella was extra playful – which always seemed to happen right after their bath – Tarra knew how to get back at her doggy friend for nipping at her feet. When the dog started nipping to see if she could get a reaction, all Tarra did was dip a shoulder to give that naughty dog an instant sand shower.

Of course Bella responded by yipping and dashing just out of reach to shake furiously as if she disliked it but Tarra knew she was faking. She could see her grinning the weird way dogs grin with their jaws apart, lips pulled back at the corners with their long pink tongues out and flapping all over the place. Such things made the elephant laugh too but elephants never show it, except maybe by an extra sparkle in their eyes. When caregivers delivered meals to the elephants wherever they were in their habitat, they always brought a dish of dog food for Bella so the two could enjoy their meals together.

In the summertime heat when it was easy for the large animals to dehydrate, the Sanctuary's water wagon drove miles through their favorite grounds to deliver water to the thirsty inhabitants. Of course Bella barked for refreshment at the same time so the water wagon always carried her blue water dish so she could drink beside Tarra.

The other elephants accepted Bella among them as though she were one of their kindred sisters. There was never a fuss as she gamboled around their large tree-trunk-sized feet. They always seemed to know that one giant misstep could end it for their dog friend, so they usually just stood still until she was out of danger.

All the other dogs in the Sanctuary surely must have

envied Bella because none of them were as welcome as she was among the elephants. Of course every elephant in the herd knew and understood the bond between that special dog and their elder sister, Tarra.

When biologist Joyce Poole had the good fortune to visit the sanctuary and see Tarra and Bella relating to each other she said that from her work with elephants and dogs she found both species were highly emotional and commonly formed close bonds. In the wild, the elephants were always living in close tight-knit groups under a female leader. They always adopted each other's young and they always mourned their dead. An animal like Tarra that had grown up with a variety of circus animals had simply continued the herds' affection which now included a dog. In fact at the time she saw the two together another stray dog was present and she said Tarra kept trying to cradle each of the dogs with her trunk. She was delighted to see this.

Interestingly, the only other creatures tolerated by the elephants as though they weren't even there were the Cattle Egrets. These large white birds followed the elephants everywhere, sometimes lightly landing on their broad gray backs and riding from pasture to pond and everywhere in between knowing that whenever the birds wanted a meal they simply took wing and flew down to the ground where the shuffling giant elephant feet always sent the flying insect population in the deep grass into a panic of fast flights.

That's just what the egrets wanted. They were experts at catching their meals in mid-air. That's why herds of elephants were always followed by flights of their feathered friends. Whenever you saw elephants moving, the insect-loving birds were always close behind. But not just elephants. They followed cows and other herd animals through grassy country for the same reason.

Tarra and Bella understood each other's moods perfectly. Whenever Bella barked and jumped around excitedly, Tarra always reached down with her trunk and rubbed it slowly along Bella's side. A sensitive finger-like extension all elephants have at the end of their trunks felt the dog to see if anything was wrong. Or perhaps it was just to pacify the dog; to re-assure her that she was all right and that her big friend was there for her. That trunk was like a friend's reassuring arm around a friend's shoulders.

Bella the dog instantly responded by leaning into that trunk and sending a signal back that she appreciated Tarra's touch. The dog let the elephant know she was alright by the responding tail thumps she gave that probing trunk when it got near. Nothing more than touching each other was all the communication they needed. Both friends understood each other perfectly.

One day when the caregivers brought Tarra her food, Bella never showed up for her blue bowl of food so she could eat with Tarra. Everyone wondered what had happened to the dog. They began searching the sanctuary for her.

Finally when they heard whining coming from a ditch, they found Bella lying there hidden by tall grass. She was trying to pull herself along with her forelegs but dragging her hind legs.

Tarra made her way to where she was and stood by as the caregivers carefully eased the whining dog onto a litter. They carried Bella to a waiting vehicle that served as an ambulance. Tarra made no effort to stop them as they carefully eased the litter into the vehicle and drove her to the sanctuary's animal hospital.

Tarra remained standing where she last saw her injured friend.

At the hospital they took X-rays of Bella and found that she had an injury to her spine that had caused the paralysis in her hind legs. There was really not much the doctors could do. They recommended that she get lots of rest and wait to see if the injury would heal itself.

A place was made for Bella in the offices over the animal barn where she would be warm. Meanwhile Tarra remained standing where she last saw her friend, waiting for her return.

Caregivers carried her food and water but made no effort to coax her away. After three days waiting, Tarra must have realized that Bella was not coming back. So it was up to her to go and find her.

The people at the sanctuary were amazed when Tarra finally left her place of vigil and slowly made her way directly to the animal barn over which Bella was now being cared for. Everyone couldn't explain how Tarra knew where her friend was, but Tarra went directly there.

Immediately, office workers knew something had happened when an exited Bella began whining and whimpering, and trying to crawl out of her bed with her forelegs. Caregivers quickly soothed her and moved her bed closer to the window so she could look down and more easily see Tarra.

Of course as soon as Tarra saw her friend all the elephants knew it because she began making her chirping sounds and then trumpeted so loudly that everyone there heard it. They knew it was Tarra, letting out a loud cheer for her grinning pal who above her was excitedly licking the window she was so happy to see her big friend.

In the days that followed Tarra and Bella carried on their long distance friendship with each other just by seeing each other. Tarra appeared each day in the same place and the two communicated as best they could through their own silent sign language.

Those who saw them knew it worked miracles in helping to heal Bella's injury. As soon as she got well enough to be moved, the caregivers carried Bella outdoors so that the two of them could be together again.

Not long after that Bella got all of the feeling and use of her hind legs back again and the doctors released her for good.

Once more the two friends were together, Bella limping quite a bit at first but every day she got better and was able to romp around with her big pal again.

Throughout this unusual friendship between Tarra and the orphaned dog Bella that had captured her heart, Carol photographed the progress of their long friendship. Then, she did something that would warm the hearts of everyone who ever heard about it.

Carol Buckley, the long-time circus performer and friend who first brought them together and who loved them both equally as much, wrote a wonderful book about their remarkable friendship. Titled, *Tarra & Bella: The Elephant and Dog who became Best Friends,* the book is filled with Carol's lovely color photographs of the two sharing fun times together. The small orphaned dog and the gigantic gray circus elephant had almost ten wonderful years doing these things together in what must have certainly seemed like animal heaven to the 36-year-old 8000-pound elephant and the 40-pound cream-colored feisty dog who befriended her.

That's the way I will always remember them; the way Carol wrote about them at the end of her book:

"Today, Bella and Tarra can be found walking side by side in the woods or napping under the shade of an ancient oak tree, Bella snuggled up close to Tarra. When they run, Bella limps, but it does not stop them from having fun. Tarra and Bella are back together, sharing their meals, their freedom and their big love. They are truly forever best friends."

CHAPTER 2

Powerful Urges Can Cause Strange Bonds

The Internet is filled with video records people have made of the bonding and friendships of some mighty strange animals. It suggests that all living creatures have an innate desire to care for other creatures no matter what species they are. Those involved seem particularly drawn to young orphans, or perhaps they have not yet matured but have the yearning to take care of some other young creature and try to mother it. When we see these things we video them because we all understand these typical maternal feelings among our own kind but sometimes are staggered by the realization that these creatures are displaying a very human emotional response that we never gave them credit for having.

Meanwhile, wherever these odd pairings occur and we witness them, we get that warm fuzzy feeling within ourselves. We may not fully understand what causes wild animals to respond in these uncommon ways but we as humans love seeing it. Possibly we are all "animal whisperers" at heart because nothing touches us so profoundly whenever we witness them.

Author Jennifer Holland writes touching stories about these unlikely relationships between different kinds of animals all over the world. Many odd pairings are often seen taking place at animal sanctuaries where caregivers often deal with orphaned and sometimes abused animals. At these wonderful havens for the lost and the needy, no richer grounds ever existed where these characteristics are so badly needed. So those caregivers are the ones who most often see animals who most desperately need love and affection in their lives. What is so marvelous is how they seek and accept it wherever they can find it, often from animals not necessarily of their own species. This interspecies relationship is extremely touching. Holland's books are charmingly written and include numerous photographs of the animal pairings she writes about.

In the following chapters I have written condensed accounts of a few of these pairings that struck me as most unusual. Despite their differences in the species of animals bonding together, the one common thing they all share is a desire to care for each other; to share the one thing most of them never had in their lives – the care and comfort usually provided by their mothers when they were very young and most in need of it. But if they are orphaned and never got that, they quickly respond in kind. It makes no difference to them that their "mom" may not look like them. The one thing they are looking for, the other creature is willing to provide.

Sometimes it is the other way around. A mother has lost her offspring and longs to "mother" a youngster of her own, no matter what it looks like! Whenever we see this in the animal world we respond sympathetically because we as humans understand only too well the need for that love in our world. Some of these samples from the animal world are lessons that tell us something about how humankind should get along together. For those who say animals have no ability to feel such emotions as love, sadness, happiness and compassion, read Jennifer Holland's books. Here are a few that touched me:

CHAPTER 3

The Leopard and the Cow

No one really knows for certain what brings about these loving bonds between animals, but those who work with them regularly in sanctuaries believe they understand what causes this between animals that would otherwise be the hunter and its prey.

Such a bond developed in a village beside a river in India. The natives were amazed to find that a leopard had crept through their sugar cane one October night and found a tethered cow where the villages usually kept their livestock at night in this dusty farming town. What fascinated these people was that this predator, that normally would have attacked and eaten the cow, did just the opposite. It bonded with the cow and each of them mutually benefited from this relationship.

Initially the villagers were quite concerned for their own safety with such a fearsome predator in their area. They asked that the Forest Department catch the leopard and place it in their nearby wildlife sanctuary.

So the professional trappers came to catch the leopard. The cat eluded them repeatedly. But that night it returned several times to visit the cow. Not as a hunter sizing up its potential supper but more as a young cat looking for affection from an animal that readily provided it. The leopard would snuggle up to the warm-bodied cow and the cow would patiently lick and clean the leopard from head to tail.

This amazed the people who saw this spectacle. Moreover it repeated itself over and over. For two months the leopard would appear about eight in the evening and snuggle up to the cow. The two would cuddle together this way all night long until sunrise. And just before sunrise, the leopard would leave for points unknown.

Once the villagers were able to see how loveable the leopard was, they were less concerned for their own safety. Not only that, but it seemed that suddenly they were less bothered by their crops being eaten by local pigs, monkeys and jackals. The villages figured that the leopard was dining on those critters and as a consequence their vegetable gardens were flourishing.

Then abruptly the cat disappeared. Nobody knew what happened. He was gone for several weeks. Whatever had happened, the two friends were not meeting any longer.

Then suddenly the leopard appeared again as if for a last tryst; a final night together. Once again they were seen cuddling at least nine separate times together with the leopard wandering off for a while and then returning to her friend. Finally that night she left for good.

So what happened here? Why was the cat so friendly for so long and then suddenly she lost interest and disappeared, never again to return to her bosom buddy?

One concerned animal expert from the sanctuary, Rohit Vyas, felt that since the young leopard had no mother it may have accidentally encountered this tethered cow who just leaned over and gave her a motherly lick. Maybe that was all it took for them to develop a closer relationship – the young cat seeking the larger cow's warmth and customary lick cleaning service that she also found pleasant. So she kept coming back and repeating the enjoyable experience.

"Eventually however," said Rohit, "perhaps the leopard matured to a point where she did more adult things and no longer required a relationship of a loving mother. So she moved on into adulthood and the two parted mutual and affectionate friends."

CHAPTER 4

The Lioness and the Antelope

Another strange animal relationship began in the National Preserve of Kenya in East Africa where large numbers of different wild animals roam free and are not encumbered by man's civilization. In this case people thought they were seeing a message from God when they saw a baby antelope lying down with a lion.

One of the anthropologists in the area quietly observed this relationship and watched over the weeks as it grew. This was the case of a fierce predator bonding to an animal that she would normally hunt. In this case the antelope was an oryx so young that it was still wobbly on its legs. It had somehow become separated from her mother. The cat was also a young lioness, too young so far to have cubs; yet old enough to recognize which animals were her prey. But for some reason she had become separated from the pride and apparently adopted the young antelope and began taking care of it as if it were her cub.

The two of them took walks together and they slept together. Those who saw her speculated that the lioness was having trouble determining whether she wanted the antelope as her cub or whether it was her meal. She licked it tenderly and regularly. Spectators decided that the mother in her took precedent over her own desires to see this animal as something she might care to eat.

Unfortunately, since young antelopes require a very rich buttery diet of their mother's milk, which the lioness could not provide, the young oryx became weakened from starvation. Still, the young lioness refused to hunt for herself because of her desire to stay and take care of her slowly weakening "cub."

At the time one of the animal specialists who observed this bond sought help from animal experts all over the world. But they too were unable to provide any suggestions because this kind of pairing simply did not occur in the wild. They all knew about cases in which young lions played with captured game for a while, but like a cat plays with a mouse it soon ceases to be a toy and becomes a meal.

But this was not occurring here. Both the oryx and the lioness were suffering because neither had the nourishment the other required and the cat refused to go hunt on her own. It looked as though both of them were slowly going to starve to death. But then, nature stepped in and resolved the problem.

The oryx had wandered away from the lioness for a short distance and a male lion simply snatched it up while the lioness was unable to do anything about it.

The very next day the cat snapped out of her lethargy and went off hunting herself a large meal consisting of a wild hog. From then on she was on her way to recovery.

But oddly enough from that moment on she did not fully respond the way a normal lion would. Those who continued to observe her reported that in the months to come this lioness adopted oryxes five more times – all for short periods – before she herself disappeared from the area, leaving behind the mystery of what the reason was for this very unusual behavior.

One can only guess. One animal behaviorist suggested that the lioness had lost her family at a critical time of her development. This may have triggered her odd obsession with these very young and likely helpless antelopes that were orphans themselves. But such behavior creates nothing but an enigma for the animal behaviorists and leaves us with a desire for the real answers to this wonderful behavior between species.

CHAPTER 5

The Monkey and the Dove

In a large wildlife preserve on an island just off the southern coast of China caretakers noticed an unusual scene – a very small baby macaque monkey had been abandoned and alone to such a degree that it was in distress and very weak. Who had come to its aid when it was taken to the sanctuary was an earlier resident – a white dove that had taken refuge there after losing its mate.

What amazed the onlookers was that the dove was attempting to care for the baby monkey. They lived together and they dined together. The baby monkey enjoyed eating kernels of corn, holding them in his tiny hands as he nibbled away. The dove followed behind him picking up fallen pieces of corn the monkey dropped. The dove cooed contentedly and the baby monkey chattered back as if they both understood each other.

At night they cuddled together in their own cage; the monkey wrapping her arms around the dove who probably wished she had arms as well. She made up for it by fluffing her feathers and making a pillow for the monkey.

Observers noted that sometimes the little macaque teased the dove by pulling on her tail feathers. The dove swiftly scolded him by pecking at his hands. They made a happy pair together. People came from all over to see how this odd couple lived together. The two so enjoyed each other and their life together that they both quickly regained their health.

This continued for quite a while but the staff at the sanctuary knew that both of them would be better off with their kind in the wild. So they set about giving them their freedom. First the dove was released and she joyfully flew off in a flash of white. The sanctuary's manager happened to revisit the place where the baby monkey was found and he was pleased to see that the macaque family had returned to the area again. He made sure that the baby was taken there to meet them and the troop immediately embraced the lost youngster. With both the dove and the baby monkey back in the wild you wonder what might happen if they should see each other again. Probably they would hug like long lost buddies as they are doing here.

MORE UNUSUAL FRIENDS

COMFY BEDFELLOWS

EVEN THEY KNOW LOVE IS BLIND

SOULMATES

Bush Baby with toy bird

It doesn't get much sweeter than this

CHAPTER 6

The Polar Bear and the Sled Dog

In northern Canada near the town of Churchill a wildlife photographer reported seeing a most unusual sight. Polar bears often scavenged the town's garbage pit for choice edibles so they were accustomed to seeing sled dogs chained beside their dog coops whenever they came foraging. The dogs, of course, raised the alarm with their excited barking whenever a polar bear came into the area.

As he watched an approaching polar bear one day the photographer noticed that one of the dogs wasn't barking. He simply stood still and watched the bear that came directly toward him.

All of a sudden the bear came up to the dog, lay down and rolled over on his back. The dog immediately leaped on the bear's belly and the two began rolling and wrestling playfully together. The big bear would hold the sled dog's head between his massive paws and the sled dog seemed to love it. He swiftly got loose by nipping the bear's hind leg. The bear in turn bit the dog's leg and did it a bit too hard. The dog yipped and the bear immediately released him.

The photographer couldn't believe what he was seeing but it was obvious that the two had done these things before and enjoyed roughhousing with each other. They played together like this for twenty minutes before the two separated.

The photographer reported seeing this happen with the same dog and polar bear several times in the next few days. Others in the area said they had seen several of the bears playing with dogs near the garbage pit. They said that sometimes these polar bears were seen running off other bears that were less affable toward the dogs.

Sadly, the locals worry that there may soon come a time when the polar bear population may no longer be there. Most of the bears live above the Artic Circle where the ice pack is declining due to the warming of the planet. It has reached the point where these animals are perishing from lack of natural food. As the Arctic's ice floes melt, so too does the seal population. If the polar bears no longer have the once large seal population to feed on, people are afraid the bears will disappear the same way as the seals.

CHAPTER 7

Dogs, People and Dolphins

Pliny the Younger (A.D. 62-113) wrote, "I have met with a story, which, although authenticated by undoubted evidence, looks very like fable…. There is in Africa a town called Hippo, situated not far from the sea coast; it stands upon a navigable lake, communicating with an estuary in the form of a river, which alternately flows into the lake or into the ocean, according to the ebb and flow of the tide…." The Roman author then went on to say that people of all ages enjoyed fishing, sailing, and swimming there, and one day, while swimming toward the opposite shore, a youngster met a dolphin which played around him and eventually allowed the boy to ride upon his back.

"The fame of this remarkable incident spread through the town, and crowds of people flocked around the boy…. The next day the shore was thronged with spectators, all attentively watching the ocean and the lake…. The dolphin appeared again and came to the boy, who together with his companions, swam away with the utmost precipitation. The dolphin as though to invite and call them back, leaped and dived up and down, in a series of circular movements.

"This he continued to do for several days until the people got brave enough to enter the water and began playing with him themselves.

"They ventured, therefore, to advance near, playing with him and calling him to them, while he in return suffered himself to be touched and stroked…. The boy, in particular, who first made the experiment, swam by the side of him, and leaping upon his back, was carried backward and forward in

"

that manner, and thought the dolphin knew him and was fond of him, while he too had grown fond of the dolphin. There seemed, now, indeed, to be no fear on either side, the confidence of the boy and the tameness of the other mutually increasing the rest of the boys in the meantime surrounding and encouraging their companion...."

Was Pliny's story fact or fable? Would wild dolphins, on their own accord, really make friends and play with humans? From a few rare incidences of a remarkably similar nature, we now know that the Roman was most likely writing the truth. Here's one example:

In September 1965, as hurricane Betsy sliced a swath across the Gulf of Mexico to sideswipe Florida, Mississippi, and Louisiana, two bottlenose dolphins seeking refuge from the storm swam through narrow Philip's Inlet into large and partially brackish Powell Lake in northwest Florida. Several days later, the badly slashed body of one of the dolphins washed ashore. Those who found it suspected it was a victim of the storm.

As usual that winter, the inlet sanded in and the lake was landlocked. Local fishermen knew that the surviving dolphin was trapped in the lake, but everyone figured it would leave in the spring when the rain-swollen lake waters pushed out the sand and opened the inlet again.

Spring came, the inlet opened, but the dolphin did not leave the lake. People began seeing it more frequently swimming near shore, as if, some said, it was searching for someone. Soon, however, the dolphin stopped searching. It had found its first friend – a dog belonging to a local fish camp.

The dog stood on its owner's dock and barked lustily at the dolphin rolling playfully in front of the dock. This continued until one-day people noticed the dog and dolphin splashing around together in the shallows near shore. The spectacle stopped grownups in their tracks. But not the kids. There was no holding them back. At first the fishing-camp children joined the dolphin and the dog in their frolicking. But soon, every youngster in the neighborhood was in on the action. Adults gathered on shore to watch and said it was quite a show – the dog, the dolphin, and all the kids whooping it up in the water together. No one ever remembered seeing anything like it before.

By summer, a kind of love affair had begun between the wild but friendly dolphin and the people of Philip's Inlet. It was not a young animal, but a nearly full-grown *Tursiops truncatus*, bottlenose dolphin. And there was no doubt the dolphin, who had lost his companion, was enjoying immensely all the attention he was getting.

That summer I heard about the dolphin from my old fishing friend, George Brown, who lived near the inlet. George had named the dolphin "Nudgy" because it liked to nudge boats until they started their motors. At an outboard's first sputter and roar, the dolphin would whip around behind the boat, and with its bottlenose inches from the spinning propeller, would follow it everywhere. Whatever the attraction was, the dolphin loved it. When the boat stopped, Nudgy tried to push it into action again. That action didn't go over too well with boat fishermen who wanted to stay where they stopped to catch fish.

At first, Nudgy's infatuation with motorboats amused most people. Others, it infuriated. Those it bothered most were anglers with their boats anchored quietly over a good fishing spot. This bumptious dolphin knocked them off, not once, but repeatedly. To the dolphin it was a delightful game.

While most of the local people understood the dolphin's playfulness and good-naturedly tolerated this bizarre behavior, many out-of-towners complained about it loudly to the fishing-camp owners. It seems that some of the fishermen's wives panicked, thinking they were under attack from a shark, which made matters worse.

After a while, when there was no letup of tourist fishermen voicing the same complaint, some of the fishing-camp owners began making complaints of their own. The dolphin was hurting business, they said. It had to go.

"Nonsense!" exclaimed almost everyone else. If anything, the dolphin was good for business. It attracted people, they argued. People came from all over to see it because it was a natural clown, one that learned tricks by itself that were just as clever as any Flipper did on television. Best of all, Nudgy was their very own! That's how most people felt around Philip's Inlet. And that's the way it went that year.

The next spring, before the tourists came, it was a different story. Some of the fishing interests on the lake got together and decided that something had to be done about the dolphin. He had to be removed. The overflowing lake had finally blown its plug at the mouth of the inlet. The molasses-brown brackish waters raced full force back into the Gulf of Mexico. What better time than the present, they reasoned, to entice the dolphin back the way he had come? After all, what self-respecting creature of the sea really wanted to live in the lake's half-fresh, tannin-stained waters when it had the whole crystal-clear Gulf of Mexico at its disposal?

Early the next morning, before the children came to play, a lone boatman pulled away from a fishing camp and gunned his powerful outboard motor raucously. Almost magically, the dolphin's sleek gray form broke the surface as it came bounding across the black-mirrored waters of the lake.

The boat roared off. Perhaps anticipating the thrill of the chase, Nudgy raced after it.

Down the lake and under the highway bridge they went, boat and dolphin, the one barely keeping ahead of the other. Nor did they slacken speed at the end of the lake where it narrowed to cut a brown swatch through the beach of sugar-white sand that had blocked the inlet all winter long.

Now, however, the channel did not meander as it would in the summer. Now it was a straight, deep, raging torrent that rushed out to blight the emerald sea with great brown splotches for miles along the coast.

Through this opening shot boatman and dolphin in tandem, the two driven even faster by the fury of the water as it formed short but violent waves at the mouth of the channel where ocean met lake. And there, in that long, uneven turbulence, the boatman lost sight of the dolphin. Still, he continued seaward, pausing only momentarily to gun his motor to make sure the dolphin heard and followed it in the stained water.

Finally, some distance from land, the boatman cut his motor to half speed and turned back, feeling sure the animal was free. Through the pass, across the end of the lake, under the bridge, and back to the fishing camp he went. Just as he tied up, he heard a commotion near shore. Glancing over, he saw two boys and a dog frolicking in the shallows with a disturbingly familiar large gray form.

In the next few weeks this scenario played again and again. Same dolphin; different boatmen. The results were always the same. Each time, the dolphin dutifully followed the boat down the lake, through the pass and out to sea. Then it impishly whirled around and beat the boat back to the dock.

The boatmen were very annoyed. The kids loved it. Almost everyone else heartily disapproved of the efforts to remove the dolphin. After all, they argued, he was their business, too. Moreover, he had made it perfectly clear that he preferred the company of people to those of his own kind. "Leave him alone!" they insisted. And they meant it.

But there seemed no way for peaceful coexistence between the fishermen and the dolphin. As the furor grew, so too did Nudgy's problems. More than once the dolphin felt the wrath of irate fishermen when his friendly bump against their boat brought him a most unfriendly bump of their oar against his dome. Soon, Nudgy's once smooth brow began to show the scrapes and scars of these encounters. But no one was really sure which were battle scars and which the result of his fascination with whirling propellers. Only once was there absolutely no doubt what had happened. Someone speared

Nudgy.

It was a shocking, unthinkable cruelty. Fortunately, the wound was superficial and soon healed. But from then on, Nudgy wore the unmistakable marks of a five-pronged fish spear on his flank. Such malice was more than anyone could understand. The only one who seemed to bear no bitterness over that unfortunate encounter was Nudgy himself.

Soon, newspapers carried accounts of the wild dolphin that had befriended the people of Philip's Inlet. As Nudgy's popularity grew, more people came to see him. Even people from the adjacent states of Georgia and Alabama made special trips to this small Florida fishing community to pay their respects to the friendly dolphin.

As his fame spread, it eventually attracted the attention of a local commercial oceanarium that kept and trained dolphins for public performances. These businessmen felt that Nudgy would be a natural attraction for their dolphin show. They came to Philips Inlet to see if this talented creature could be caught and persuaded to go professional; joining the ranks of other captive dolphins that daily entertained crowds of people in exchange for free room and board.

Of course, there was no way to tell Nudgy that if he went professional he would never have to hunt for food as long as he lived. But would the hard-working fishing folk of Philip's Inlet understand the practicality of this arrangement?

Indeed they did. The people of Philip's Inlet understood perfectly. For the first time – some perhaps more reluctantly than others – both the pro-dolphin and-the anti-dolphin people agreed. The dolphin was free to go wherever it wanted, but no one, they vowed, would ever take Nudgy away from them and turn him into a circus performer they had to pay to see. Not their freedom-loving dolphin.

Once or twice it seemed that some litigation might arise over the issue of who owned the wild dolphin and who had the right to claim it. But in the end the dolphin lovers of Philip's Inlet settled the issue through sheer determination.

One sunny afternoon I drove to the coast to catch Nudgy's performance. As usual, it was an informal affair, taking place in the shallow water near shore where the youngsters cavorted with the big gray dolphin while the adults stood in the shade of the loblolly pines watching the fun. Since I wanted to take pictures of the activities, I asked the kids to play close to a dock where I could look down on the action and photograph it.

Nudgy was on his best behavior. On cue from a suddenly started outboard motor, he shot across the intervening water to hover in a state of almost unrestrained excitement behind the idling motor, as if daring it to go. When it was slipped into gear, the boat leaped away with the dolphin seemingly glued by the end of its nose to the spinning propeller. Around and around they went in tight circles until the motorboat sputtered to a stop. With an adroit lift of his head, Nudgy tipped the foot of the motor out of water and the crowd applauded.

Closer to shore, a small boy summoned the dolphin for more fun and games by sticking the brass bell of an old taxi horn in the water and squeezing the rubber bulb to make it squawk.

Nudgy streaked back to the kids, flipped over on his back, and swam circles around them upside down. The shore crowd cheered. As if taking a bow, Nudgy righted himself, swam between a youngster's legs, then surfaced to roll on top of the water in the middle of the group to accept good-naturedly the children's hands that patted him in praise of his fine performance. This kind of activity went on for the rest of the afternoon. Everyone seemed to be having a wonderful time. Especially the star performer.

Several months passed before I got down to the coast to see Nudgy again. But I kept track of his activities through short notes from my friend George. Once again trouble sprang up between Nudgy and the fishermen. Then abruptly, everything quieted down. I heard nothing from George.

Finally, after a while, I drove to the inlet to see what was happening. When I saw the dolphin, I knew things had changed. The fishing-camp owner whose dog and children had first befriended him now kept Nudgy in an enclosure bounded by docks. It was a kind of pen about thirty feet square. All that really confined the dolphin in that shallow water was a chicken-wire fence strung around the dock pilings. The dolphin could easily leap over the low structure and escape whenever he wished. But apparently he chose not to do so.

I learned that the owner let him out at night to feed in the lake; he returned of his own accord. During the day he always stayed inside the enclosure. Surely, the fishermen had no complaints about this arrangement.

With other visitors, I walked out on the dock to see the dolphin. Instead of swimming around inside his pen as I had expected, Nudgy stayed away from the sides, remaining more in the middle of the enclosure, warily eyeing the people on the dock. Some children splashed water, trying to coax him closer so they could pet him. But the dolphin kept his distance, periodically lifting his head to breathe while watching the onlookers.

Only once did I see him respond to a spectator. An older boy tossed several pebbles toward him to attract his attention. Nudgy responded by lifting his head and squirting a sizable stream of water straight at his tormentor, scoring a direct hit. Everyone but the boy laughed. Then the crowd quickly dispersed. Most took it to mean that Nudgy was simply in no mood to play.

After the spectators left, I stood on the dock watching the dolphin. I felt depressed. It was not a happy scene. I had enjoyed seeing Nudgy free. Seeing him there by himself in the muddy water of his chicken-wire pen seemed wrong, even if he could come and go whenever he wished. Perhaps it was only my imagination, but at that moment I had the distinct impression that the dolphin's perpetual smile was no longer there.

I never saw the dolphin again after that. Several weeks later, George sent me a short note. All it said was, "We lost Nudgy last night."

I never asked what happened. I do not want to know. I would rather believe that one night when he went out to feed, Nudgy just kept going down the lake, under the bridge, through the inlet, and out to sea to play with his family and friends, where all dolphins belong.

CHAPTER 8

My Affair with Mermaids

Columbus reported seeing some of their early family members in 1493, less than three months after he first sighted the New World. His chronicler wrote: "Wednesday the ninth of January…when the Admiral (Christopher Columbus) went to the River of Gold, he saw three mermaids…they were not as beautiful as they are painted though they have something like the human face. He said he had seen some before off the coast of Guinea…."

Columbus's mermaids are believed to have been the West Indian manatee (*Trichechus manatus*), the serene marine mammal also called a sea cow. Even after Columbus, certain nearsighted seventeenth-century sailors still thought they were mermaids. But one suspects that, like Columbus, they had been too long at sea. Sea cow, a name acquired more recently, links these animals with their very earliest prehistoric ancestors, the elephants. Animal genealogy experts believe that one member of the elephant family apparently ran off to sea and never came ashore again. Certain manatee skeletal similarities link them to elephants. With an order name like *Sirenia*, from the Latin *Siren*, one wonders if these are the sirens sailors have been harking to ever since Ulysses' time.

I met my first manatee when I was diving near the main spring at Crystal River, Florida. Suddenly, there she was, suspended in mid-water like a huge gray barrage balloon with wave shadows dappling her back. Though she was alone, I knew others were in the area because it was a cold winter day with freezing air temperatures. The water temperature, as customary with all Florida springs, was about 68 degrees. I was comfortable in my wet suit. So were the manatees that annually winter there because of this warm water environment. As air-breathing mammals they are susceptible to catching pneumonia in cold weather. From years of experience they know that Florida's coastal bays that contain copiously flowing freshwater springs will keep them comfortable and healthy until warmer weather arrives enabling them to continue their coastal wanderings. It is in these springs during these winter months that men and manatees meet, sometimes for the first time.

My appearance seemed to startle this large female as much as hers did me. We both stopped swimming and eyed each other suspiciously, waiting for the other to react. As I learned later, this manatee had met divers before and her response was typical. Are you friend or foe she seemed to question. Divers recognize different manatees by the patterns of their sliced and macerated broad flat tails, damage from accidental encounters with boat propellers. Most coastal manatees have these disfiguring cuts. This one's cuts identified her as a female named Sadie. When she saw me, she appeared shy, turning her big frame side-ways while watching me out the corner of her tiny eye.

Abruptly, scurrying around from behind her appeared a miniature version of Sadie, a wrinkle-faced youngster gamboling through the water like a playful colt. About the size of one too. I suspected it was Sadie's calf. Without the slightest apprehension, the youngster came up to me and playfully nuzzled the coiled cord of my underwater camera strobe. I reached out and petted her. She in turn arched her back, seemingly enjoying it. Looking away from Sadie I scratched the calf under her chin. Like a puppy, she promptly rolled over on her side to give me more of her to scratch.

At that moment something nudged me from behind. Sadie was at my shoulder. She pushed her bucket-sized head against me again, then backed off as though wondering how I would react to her boldness. Her nudge seemed friendly, but she was cautious about coming any closer. I had a feeling she was not quite sure how I would respond. She seemed shy but anxious for attention.

The moment I reached out and touched her, whatever shyness she may have felt immediately vanished. As she drew closer so I could pet and rub her almost hairless, rather tough hide, her all-seeing tiny eyes closed tightly. It was no stretch of my imagination to see that she was luxuriating in the gentle massage I was giving her jowls. Then, almost in slow motion, this great, grayish, round dirigible beside me slowly started rolling over. It was like watching a ponderous iceberg turn bottom-side up.

The feat finally accomplished, Sadie lay belly up on her back before me, displaying her ample charms for all and sundry to see. I rubbed my hand across her chest several times; then caressed her flanks. Her whole body seemed to shudder deliciously. I wondered if I had tickled her. My hand moved back to her ample bosom. Sadie seemed to stretch out even more, if this were possible. Her head was thrown back so I could tickle the bristly triple chins beneath her bewhiskered lip pads. Then, as I slid back to that broad bosom again, she did something unexpected.

As I rubbed her chest, her two big flippers, which manatees use like hands, reached up and pressed my hand to her chest. It startled me because it was so unexpected. Did she want me to stop rubbing, or did she like it so much she wanted me to keep my hand where it was? I was a bit helpless because my left hand clutched camera and strobe. With my free hand clasped tightly to her chest, Sadie slowly started to roll away from me. As she did, I was forced to go with her.

It was a weird sensation because she was pulling me up and over the side of her huge body. Since I was using just mask and snorkel, a vision flashed through my mind of how this bizarre turn of events might end up – with me on the bottom beneath this two thousand-pound oddly behaving female sea cow. Not my idea of fun.

But she had clasped me so tightly that it took all I could do to pull my hand free before she accomplished whatever it was she had in mind. Then she did the ponderous iceberg trick again, rolling right side up, a mischievous look in her eyes.

Again I patted her on the head; then a tickle and Sadie rolled over upside down once more. After a brisk belly rub ending at her chest, she once more pinned my hand and began the slow roll – never toward me always away from me. This time I had to find out what would happen. I decided to go along for the ride. It wasn't as bad a trip as I had imagined.

I just went up and over, then under, with Sadie settling down on top of me. I reached up and pushed her elephantine body away from me with no difficulty. She might weigh a couple tons out of the water but underwater her blubber and lung capacity made her amazingly buoyant. This explained how these large mammals bounce in slow motion to the surface periodically to breathe and make it look so effortless.

Later I learned that all of these things were the way Sadie greets everyone. No exceptions. Once she is sure you mean her no harm, she does her thing. Whenever we met – and we had these clandestine meetings several times a year for three years – it was always the same.

Sadie and I became great friends. She was always playful and anxious to please. Often we swam side by side. If I stopped, she stopped. If I held out my hand, she would put her flipper in it. I would then draw her near to take a close-up photograph of her. Each time the camera shutter clicked, Sadie-blinked. She could clearly hear the almost inaudible sound, one apparently not so inaudible to her because, each time it happened, she flinched. This told me how sensitive her hearing was. Though it did not otherwise seem to annoy her, after each picture-taking session I would usually put the camera equipment aside and become more involved in developing a relationship with her.

In all our slow, gentle touching and tumbling together, Sadie's calf stayed close to us, occasionally begging for attention, too. It was almost impossible to devote full time to belly-rubbing the upside-down mother without also having to pacify the little calf jostling beside us. Occasionally, however, the calf would go off to play with the other manatees in the area. Or it would simply settle to the bottom and contentedly graze in the thick pastures of hydrilla weed that grows abundantly on the bottom of Crystal River. The herbivorous mammals sometimes literally eat themselves into caves of this vegetation, then fall asleep right where they are. Naps are seldom more than five or ten minutes; the mammal surfaces to breathe and then returns to the lush green pastures for another few minutes rest. Manatees can hold their breaths for up to fifteen minutes.

Sometimes while swimming with Sadie, I purposely fell behind to watch her. Her large flat tail had been slashed into three separate pieces by a boat's whirling propeller. The accident may have occurred on an occasion when she surfaced to breathe. Similar marks and cuts appear on the backs of most of the slow-moving mammals. Ironically, these livid white scars, often resembling the serpentine pattern of the trail of a sidewinder rattlesnake across a sandy desert, help divers and scientists identify the various manatees.

Usually, when I fell behind and Sadie realized I was missing, she would stop swimming and wait for me to catch up. If I failed to appear she would then turn around to see where I was. Sadie accomplished this operation by paddling vigorously with one flipper until her great body slowly pivoted around and she could see where I was. If I still remained there and she saw I was not coming, she would then swim back to join me. With one sweep of her broad tail she was quickly beside me, peering quizzically into my mask as if to ask, "What's wrong?"

Manatees are very adroit with their flippers. Not only do they use them independently to help them move about in the water their flippers help bring food to the animal's mouth and in this sense are used as crude hands. You can feel fingerlike bones within the flipper, which possess nails that look much like elephant toenails. These features suggest their land animal heritage say the experts.

Often we see manatees pushing their large lip pads and cheeks with their flippers, apparently in an effort to dislodge a piece of vegetation caught between their teeth. Most of the animals are too apprehensive about allowing a diver to place his hand near their mouth or face; however, one young sea cow I met relished this kind of contact.

It was initiated by her coming up and kissing me full on my facemask. In the process, she placed both flippers on each side of my head to accomplish it. I, in response, reached out and placed my hands on each side of her head and gently stroked her cheeks. I was rubbing her whiskers and had worked down around her thick lip pads when she started nibbling on my fingers. Not sure if I was ready yet to be gummed by a nibble-happy calf, I held up my hand flat in front of her face and she continued nibbling my palm. Her prehensile lips reached out, curled over my fingertips and held my hand firmly in place where she could nibble better.

This particular calf enjoyed all manner of petting and was fond of being touched and rubbed, especially around her flippers and under her jowls. Sometimes she would head for the bottom in a series of spirals, and then come back to the surface to see where I was. Unlike some manatees, she enjoyed making close frontal contact. One area that seemed in particular to please her was under the apex of her flippers. If there is any sexual connotation to the man/manatee relationship, part of it may stem from this particular caress, for the apex of the flipper is where the nipple is located, one on each side, and where the female suckles its young. The nipples are capable of erection, which occurs when a diver touches them. Not all female manatees solicit this caress, but most do, and the contact is quite obviously pleasurable for them.

The last winter I visited the sea cows I had my most memorable experience. That morning my wiper blades froze to the windshield, the car was coated with ice, and at nine A.M. as I slid into the water near the spring, the air was so cold the water smoked.

It was the day after Christmas and north Florida was weathering a cold snap. That night the mercury had nose-dived into the twenties. I figured the manatees would be bunched up in the spring and it looked like a good day for relating with them.

Mask and snorkel adjusted, camera and strobe ready, I finned away from my boat and watched the brown rocks and hydrilla slide past below my mask. First the hydrilla disappeared, leaving only the rugged bare rocks; then they too vanished, leaving only the deep green void of the spring.

From its sun-splintered depths, a school of jacks drifted up in a slow-motion swirl of silver shapes, riding an up-current from the spring cave that fractured the cliff face thirty feet below.

I paused to watch their unhurried ballet before moving on across the deep pool. Just as I reached the buttressing boulders on the far side, I saw my first swimming companion of the day: a half-grown manatee wedging herself beneath the broad shoulders of a bottom fissure, rubbing her flanks lazily against the rocks and her stomach on the soft sand bottom. At first I failed to understand what she was doing. Then I saw that she had placed herself precisely in the middle of the spring run and was luxuriating in the warm water flowing past her from the spring pool.

As I drifted down the run, looking into the distance, I saw several manatees emerging from the green-amber murk. Three appeared on my left, all adults. Then two calves and a female emerged to my right. Several more shapes materialized behind them. It looked like quite a herd.

When they saw me they swam over to investigate. They

encircled me, large and small alike, cheek by jowl with each other, their tiny button eyes winking as they looked me over. The calves were more curious and less cautious than their elders, as usual, moving in close as if to sniff me out.

"Hello!" I burbled through my snorkel, holding out my hand to them. "Hello, you marvelous mermaids!"

They responded by moving closer. Before I knew it, calves, cows, and bulls were crowding me from all directions. I felt like a traffic cop caught in a busy intersection with a broken traffic light. The herd apparently accepted my presence without a second thought, for at one point I was wedged tightly between three animals and found myself from necessity studying at close range the evenly spaced sensor-like hairs standing straight up on a pair of broad backs. Enough algae grew in patches further back to attract a pair of hungry sheepshead. In their eagerness, one fish nipped a cow's back harder than usual and instantly – one apparently frightening the other – both manatees bucked furiously away from the finny molesters, much to my relief.

With the traffic jam cleared, I turned to find a friendly calf hanging at my elbow as if waiting patiently for some attention. Slowly, I reached out and petted his wrinkled hide. Here was another animal with this odd skin condition that makes them look older than their years. The hide was creased and wrinkled as if with age. Some of the calves are often so wrinkled from one end to the other that they resemble woolly sheep.

After photographing the youngster nibbling my fingertips, I moved back among the elders and began snapping pictures; recording a variety of back scars I had never seen before. Moving in among the mammals, I noticed one in particular that kept following me.

Finally, I turned to snap her picture, and then was shocked to see she had but one flipper. The other had been neatly severed just ahead of the teat. How, I wondered? A boat propeller, nylon fish line, shark, or alligator? All were there in the river, even sometimes, sharks (I was told) that sometimes venture into this fresh and brackish waterway from the Gulf of Mexico. A ragged laceration would suggest a shark perhaps. But the clean amputation suggested that it happened from a sudden encounter with a fisherman's trolled monofilament line, which in an instant can slice deeply into a sailboat's fiberglass rudder before the line breaks. A flipper would simply disappear. The rest of the manatee's body was surprisingly free of any other marks.

To assist in my examination of her, she obligingly rolled belly up. I patted her chest. She reached up with her one good flipper and pressed my hand to her bosom. It was a simple, touching gesture. After a while, my left hand holding camera and strobe began to cramp. When I tried to withdraw, she clamped down tighter. Shades of Sadie I thought, thankful that at least she wasn't trying to roll me. Tugging only drew her to me.

Somehow we ended up in a kind of cheek-to-cheek embrace. And she still had my hand. Curious to see just how long she would tolerate this familiarity, I started swimming her around on her back. She seemed charmed. Her head back, eyes closed, a slight "smile" on her lips, she struck me as looking terribly anthropomorphically content with herself. Together we waltzed around the spring run together. It would have made quite a picture. The rest of the herd acted as if we were something they saw every day. Either that or they were too blasé to look.

After a while, I was the one to break the embrace. My cooperative partner rolled upright and seemed satisfied to lead me back toward the main herd. I followed beside her. As long as I stayed there where she could feel my presence, she kept swimming. Once, however, when I stopped to take a photograph of her from behind and she got ahead. I saw her stop; look right, then left, trying to spot me. Then, vigorously, her one good flipper began pulling at the water. Slowly she turned around until her little eyes caught sight of me. Then, like an overgrown puppy, she bounded back to my side. Only later, after I had slipped back across the main spring to my boat to change film, did I momentarily lose sight of her.

But later that afternoon when other divers appeared, I saw the calf again. She nuzzled me for attention so I put my camera aside and began petting her. In a moment another diver in a bright blue dive suit appeared beside me and also began petting the calf with but one flipper. I immediately backed off so that the new diver could enjoy the experience. Only then did I realize that the diver was a girl. But what caught my eye was the fact that her right arm sleeve was folded up and clipped off. She had but one hand to pet this one-flipper calf. I got a lump in my throat.

Returning to the spring run again, I encountered my old friend Sadie and her calf. It was a nice reunion. While I was playing with her calf, Sadie watched me soulfully. Finally, she nudged my shoulder for a little affection, too. Reaching out, I petted her head. That's all it took and my friendly dirigible turned bottom-side up. But the ploy didn't work this time. I had had enough handholding. When she saw I would not play her game, Sadie rolled right-side up, eyeing me as mischievously as ever. With a friendly pat on the head and a final tickle of her chins, I waved good-bye to Sadie and finned off to see what was happening with the others.

The herd grazed contentedly in the thick pastures of aquatic weeds growing beside the sandy run. I watched and photographed them for several hours, occasionally taking time to play with the friendly calves or with my one-flipper friend.

At about two P.M. I witnessed a sight few people have ever been privileged to see before. Three manatees I had not seen earlier swam into the run. A large female followed by a young male. Tagging between them came a calf belonging to the female. The persistent male kept nuzzling the female. She in turn seemed willing to accept his advances. Before long, she pushed her muzzle into the soft sand bottom, lifted her tail toward the surface at a forty-five-degree angle and the male, approaching from behind; wrapped himself about her for the conjugal embrace. The two remained in this position for seven minutes; then separated, both surfacing briefly for a breath of air. Immediately afterward they resumed their embrace and this activity, periodically interrupted for breathing, continued for the next hour.

Meanwhile, the female's calf remained nearby, never straying more than a few feet away from its mother. Sometimes it sidled up beside the mating pair as if seeking attention. After nuzzling the mother's flanks several times, the baby got what it wanted. In the act of mating, the mother shifted her flipper and the offspring eagerly pushed its muzzle over the exposed teat and commenced nursing.

For me, this scene summed it all up. Here was everything man had come to love about these marvelous mammals. Here was caring and sharing, playfulness and peace. Here was *Sirenia*, the mermaids of mythology, their silent siren song coming through loud and clear.

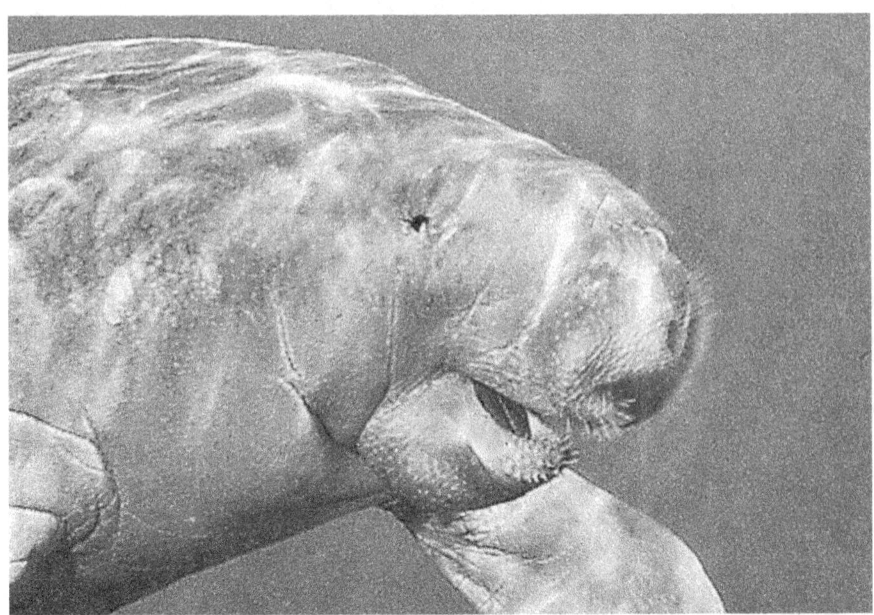

CHAPTER 9

The Man Who Befriended a Crocodile

One cool foggy morning in 1989 Costa Rica commercial fisherman Gilberto Shedder, known locally as Chito, headed upriver in his boat to fish the Parismina River. These were familiar waters to him since he lived in nearby Siquirres, and fished them every day. As did other commercial fishermen like him, he started out with his boat at first light because that was the best time to catch fish.

Chito always maneuvered his way far up this brackish river and then he fished it back riding the current all the way catching silvery white sweet-tasting fish we know as snook. The Costa Ricans called them *róbalos*. These fish were always much in demand in the local fish markets because they tasted so good. And as he did every day along this long, winding river on its way to the sea, he liked to watch the banks for crocodiles. By doing that he learned their habits. He liked crocs. He thought they were neat. He wished he could befriend one.

As the sun came out so did the big crocodiles crawling out on sandbars or on low banks where they could catch the rays of the rising sun. Chito knew that as the sun rose from the east the crocs were quick to find places along the western bank of the river so they could catch those first warm rays.

Unlike most people, Chito had a fondness for these fearsome looking reptiles. He knew that they had a bad reputation all over the world but these creatures fascinated him. He wondered if such a creature could ever be tamed.

Understandably they always ran from men because they were afraid of them. Man never showed these dangerous animals any kindness. How would they relate to him if he didn't scare them away? Could he ever get one of them to accept him as a friend without the croc trying to eat him? What a marvelous thing that would be!

As part of his daily fishing routine along the river, Chito also tried to be friends with the local crocodiles. He figured that if they ever could accept him as someone not to be afraid of, maybe they would be less likely to attack him if he accidentally fell off his boat into the water.

He often tried approaching a sunning crocodile slowly while he talked very quietly and soothingly to them, holding out a tempting gift of fresh fish. After several months a couple of the scaly sunbathing giants finally allowed him to actually approach close enough let him touch their thick scaly hides. After that, however, they usually bolted and made a massive, frantic dive back into the safety of their red-mud-colored brackish river.

Earlier on this particular morning Chito had noticed a smaller crocodile resting on the bank just below a farm that had grazing cattle. He noticed it in the early morning and was surprised to see him still there in the late afternoon on his way home. Most of the other crocs were now on the eastern shore enjoying the warm rays from the setting sun.

Chito eased his boat toward the croc that was now on the shaded side of the river. He talked soothingly and held out a large chunk of fish toward him.

The croc never moved. As Chito eased closer he realized something was wrong with him. He thought maybe he was sick because he never moved at all. Also Chito saw how emaciated he was; then he realized why when he saw the dried blood. The croc had been shot in his left eye. Chito learned later the farmer with the cattle took pot shots at all crocs he saw because they were attacking his calves.

But this one was no longer able to do that. It was obvious

that he was dying. He was too weak to even push himself into the water any longer.

Chito immediately felt sorry for the wounded animal. He had lost so much weight that despite his length of three-meters he probably weighed only about 150 pounds. Chito felt sure that if he could get him back to his place he could maybe nurse him back to health. But as it was he was too heavy for Chito to get aboard his boat. He needed help.

Chito knew where to get that. He hailed fishermen friends of his that, like hisself were going home on the river for the night.

Several immediately pulled their boats over and joined him. When they learned what he wanted them to do they told him he was crazy. But they knew Chito always had a soft spot for injured animals so they agreed to help him. Before they touched the croc however, to be sure the injured animal wouldn't bite the hands that were helping it, they wrapped a rope snugly around his powerful jaws so he couldn't open them. Then, together they lifted the crocodile and placed it in Chito's boat. The wounded animal never resisted.

"He was a little irritated," said Chito, "but he didn't have much strength he was so skinny."

The men knew the croc was closer to death than life and if he lasted the night it would be a miracle.

At the boat landing they moved the croc into the back of Chito's pick-up truck and followed him home. They unloaded the wounded croc in a place Chito fixed for him beside a manmade lake in his front yard. When Chito's wife saw what her husband and his friends had brought home with him, she threw up her hands and ran into their house, letting the screen-door slam loudly behind her.

Whether or not the wounded crocodile lived or died was now up to the Lord. They both prayed on it. While Chito's wife asked the Lord to please make her husband come back to his senses, Chito prayed that the wounded animal might be allowed to live. He promised the Lord that if he could make it

through the night, Chito would do everything he could to
nurse him back to health so he could release him back into the
wild again.

Apparently nobody upstairs listened to his wife's prayer
because the next morning Chito was just as croc-crazy as ever.
But the fisherman's prayer apparently was well received
because the crocodile was still alive the next morning. Chito
was so pleased that he named his injured friend, "Pocho,"
which he said meant "a big, strong handsome guy."

For the next three months Chito worked with his rescued
crocodile, in the beginning encouraging him to eat so he could
get strong again. When Pocho showed no interest in food,
Chito got down where he could see him and mimicked eating
a piece of chicken or fish, saying "Ummmm, so good, Pocho"
then he pretended to take a bite of raw fish and chew it up
enticingly.

Gradually Pocho began to respond to his tender
encouragement. And once he got the crocodile to eating what
was offered to him, he got the medicine the local vet gave
Chito to slip in with the food that would make him well.

"When I touched him, he would sometimes get a little
irritated," said Chito, "so I kept on petting and caressing him.
And I would say, "Relax, relax. I want to be your friend.
Behave nicely 'cause you won't be bothered anymore."

Chito spent all the time he could coddling his crocodile,
which seemed to understand what Chito was doing for him.
Pocho may have understood but Chito's wife didn't. She said
that Chito thought more of this man-eater than he did of her.
And that he was spending all of his free time with Pocho and
neglecting her.

"My family was very upset," said Chito. "My family
didn't want for me to have it there. Everyone was scared since
it was big and skinny and ugly. Everyone would say that I
was crazy and asked how can I do this with this animal? It
might eat my one-year-old daughter and my family. I almost

lost my family, my sister, my brother, because they wouldn't come here anymore. But I didn't want to take him to the river because he was injured, you know."

When his wife saw the months pass and Chito still spent more time with his crocodile, than he did with her, she left him.

Chito regretted her choice but he just shrugged and said, "Any man can get another wife, but he can't get a loveable crocodile like Pocho." He felt he was the most unusual crocodile in the whole world. Chito was teaching him to love man rather than be afraid of him. To Chito that was the Lord's miracle. No one in the whole world had ever done such a thing before and probably never would again. As soon as he knew the croc would live Chito went into town and got the necessary government papers that would allow him to work with the crocodile. He also talked to a vet who prescribed medicine for him.

It took Chito three months to see any change for the better but it was three years before he was fully well. After that, Pocho grew amazing fast. He was no longer a frail dying sad accident that man tried to destroy. He was now a sixteen-foot long, very big guy. Chito never tired of telling him that.

So, when Pocho was finally healthy again, Chito did what he intended to do in the first place. He backed his battered red truck up to his lake and with food samples along the way he enticed the big crocodile up a wide wood ramp until he was in the bed of the truck. Then, tucking Pocho's long tail in with him he closed the tailgate and in a cloud of red dust he drove the croc back to the river where he came from.

Once again he coaxed the big croc down the wood ramp and into the river.

"Goodbye, Pocho, Have a good life my handsome friend. I will miss you." He waved at Pocho, giving him the hand sign he always used when they parted for the night. Tears ran freely down Chito's dusty cheeks. He knew he was losing a friend unlike any he had ever had before.

Pocho sat in the shallow water at the edge of the river looking back at Chito. He didn't know what was happening. He thought soon that Chito would wade into the water, put his head down close to his and talk their love talk that they alone understood.

But Chito couldn't make himself do that. It was hard enough this way. Without looking back at him, the fisherman drove off in a cloud of red dust. A perplexed Pocho just stared after him.

It wasn't far to his small modest stucco house. The house was very quiet. Chito sat down on his veranda in an old beach chair he had found and stared at his empty lake. There were no ripples now where Pocho used to hunker down into the mud there and make vibrations from deep inside of him. Chito knew what he was doing. He was calling to any female that might have come into the swamp at the end of the lake where the water came from.

The deep rumbling sound always made Chito sad because he knew that Pocho was lonely. He was calling to any female that might have found their way into his swamp. But none ever answered.

Chito sat on his veranda watching the sunset. He was not hungry. He just wanted to sleep. He wondered if he should go fishing the next morning. He had missed a number of days and he needed the money. Maybe too he had better go to Mass come Sunday. Like Pocho he might get lucky and find himself a new wife there.

Next morning he awoke and still groggy he brewed himself a tin cup of strong black coffee. A couple gulps of that cleared the cobwebs out of his head. As he glanced toward the lake he suddenly froze.

Pocho was lying on the veranda comfortably stretched out waiting for him. As Chito gasped he saw a twinkle like a spark in his one good eye and whether you believe it or not he realized that the croc's partly opened mouth showing all of his sharp ivory teeth and that one good eye made him think the croc was grinning at him. And of course, that's exactly what Pocho was doing.

Not believing that the crocodile really preferred staying with him rather than living free in the wild, Chito drove the croc back to the river two more times. And each morning there he was lying on his veranda again.

After that Chito and Pocho were almost inseparable. Pocho was sixteen feet long now and had a huge girth. The two very different friends played together in the water like adolescents, Chito constantly talked in a soft, soothing voice to the crocodile, telling him what a big handsome guy he was and how much Chito loved him.

Whenever they were apart the croc always came to him when Chito called his name. That told Chito that the croc could be trained, so he began teaching him a routine that the two of them did together in the water. Chito called it their dance together. Chito taught Pocho simple tricks. He would roll over on command, lift his tail out of water and let Chito put his head in his mouth. Other times they wrestled together turning over and over together in the water. Chito would dive under the croc and come up lifting his whole head and forelegs out of water. Other times Pocho circled around the lake with Chito riding on his back.

They always seemed able to read each other's wishes by watching each other's eyes. Without being too aware of it, Chito constantly used hand signals to get Pocho to do something for him. Sometimes when they were in the water together, Pocho would open his impressive jaws real wide and swim swiftly toward Chito as if to frighten him but Chito knew he would always close those jaws before the croc reached him. When he did things like that to tease Chito, the fisherman always saw his mouth drawn back at the corners as though Pocho was laughing at him. That's when Chito would reach out, lift the croc's snout up and plant a kiss on the tip of his nose.

When someone saw the man and crocodile swimming together it wasn't long before a reporter appeared to see if this rumor was true. What he saw no man had ever seen before. When the reporter asked Chito what made him think he could befriend a wild crocodile, Chito said, "I just wanted him to feel that someone loved him; that not all humans are bad. I love all animals, especially ones that have suffered."

Once the story of the man who had befriended a crocodile became known, people from all over came to see this incredible feat. The two began putting on performances in the man-made lake in front of Chito's house. The crowds cheered their remarkable act. Those who knew crocodiles speculated that since this was an American crocodile these were thought to be shyer and less aggressive than other of the world's crocodiles. Perhaps that was why this bond was possible. No one had heard of such a thing ever happening anywhere before.

In July 2000, Costa Rica's Channel 7 filmed the unusual pair. Almost overnight Chito and Pocho became stars, receiving attention as far as the United States, Chile and the United Kingdom.

One day when a writer for an important magazine came to take pictures of the two friends, the man asked a lot of questions. Chito answered them as best he could.

"How do you do what you do with this fierce looking crocodile?" asked the man.

Chito told him that during the long time it took to nurse the crocodile back to good health that they just bonded and the friendship developed after that.

"I gave myself totally to Pocho," said Chito. "It's a feeling like when I go to sleep. I feel very calm. When the night comes and I join him in the water I feel at peace in the natural warmth between us. When a full moon is out, that's when it is perfect for us. It is a time when I am most alert because all the other animals are very active. It is the hunting time. The worst time is when it thunders. He gets out of the water. I think he knows lightning is dangerous.

"Pocho is so clever this time of night. When the moon is full and the lake is calm we do our dance. We hold tight to each other and we roll and play in the moonlight. For me it is like being with God. Nighttime is when crocodiles are the most aggressive, but not Pocho. I can tell from the feel of his body when he is tense and nervous. But he is not tense on those nights; he is just relaxed and happy. Even my daughter, Shapera, loves him. And so does my second wife. She does not mind the time I spend with my friend. Pocho is just one of the family.

"When I am alone with Pocho I feel like an animal. Often I think back to his injury, how we had to heal it. I feel completely connected to Pocho. I am part of the nature of this animal. I gave him food when he was dying but he needed more. He needed my love. I wasn't sure how close to get. It took me awhile to understand the signs he now gives me. I slowly start to touch him and he never tries to bite me. Once he recovered his strength I was expecting him to go back to the wild. He was afraid to go. He decided to stay. That's when the trust grew stronger and then I began to move closer to him. I was scared when he went crazy and threw me off his back. Then I learned to read his moods.

"So much of his feelings are in his eyes. When Pocho is anxious you can see a lot of blinking in his eyes. His eyes blink. When he is happy his eyes are normal. I can tell easy because I look at his eyes every day.

"He loves me. He also watches my eyes. I communicate with my eyes that I do not want to hurt him.

"Now he comes to me. He doesn't attack me but he likes to touch me with his body. He sends me signals when he is happy and restrained when he is agitated. We have this routine of movements we created over the years. In our dance if I give one of the moves he doesn't like he won't cooperate. That's when I have to go back and do the movement again. And after that he is happy again. I never push him. I only try things twice. If he doesn't do it I leave him. You can't push a thousand pound animal around."

The writer/photographer wrote: "When you first see this [how he behaves with Chito] you immediately think that this is impossible and then of course you start to think as a human-being. You try and think of some kind of rational explanation for it and then the first thing that comes to mind of course is that it is a feeding dependency. But there are periods of time when he doesn't feed the animal up to three weeks and yet the animal still comes to him. It does not seem to think out that connection, that interaction with him."

Chito went on to explain: "When I give him food I hit him with the fish so he associates that feeling with biting and eating. When I touch him with my hand I touch him gently so that he knows it isn't food, and won't bite me. He gets excited when I go in the water. He loves to touch; he loves to play. If I had to go away for a few days, he gets agitated. He waits for me. He doesn't bite me because he respects me.

"And," wrote the writer, "one starts to wonder if Pocho reacts to all people like he does to Chito. There is only one way to find out...."

With Chito's permission the brave writer nervously got in the water with the two of them. Chito asked him to take off his shirt because that was the way he was use to seeing Chito.

"The first time I got in the water with Chito and Pocho" he wrote, "I was really relying on Chito to put hisself between me and the croc at all times and minimize the risk of attack. The only other person that got into the water with him had his leg broken when the animal lashed out with his tail. I needed to be really careful. I'm starting to get a richer picture of the language of all crocodiles when they move their eyes rapidly and they arch their backs. This generally means they are feeling very aggressive or threatened. They are also incredibly sensitive to any sound or vibration and they can pick it up over very large distances. So I needed to be very conscious of what I was doing when I was in the water."

Chito also told the writer that crocs were very sensitive to smell and that they built up associations with various things in their environment that they smell through pheromones [a chemical an animal produces which changes the behavior of another animal of the same species].

"But it got quite hairy at times," wrote the writer, "when I could sense the croc wanted to come in and I had to trust his ability to have a real good read of the situation. I started to put the camera down and get into the water with the animal without Chito being a barrier between me and that animal. I'd learned the easy things. I'd learned to watch for the arching back and agitation. But the critical thing that I needed to do was to get in the water and actually get close to the animal.

"Can a croc feel your emotions?" asked Chito. "Yes, he can feel them."

"When Chito is working with Pocho he is constantly talking to him as if he is talking to a human and what's more important than the words themselves is the way they are spoken…I'm really trying to control my fear.

"As I approached the croc and held his tail from behind he immediately reacted and swam off. He really was not happy with my presence in the water. The arched tail in croc language indicated he wasn't interested because it clearly indicated the relationship was between Chito and the animal and that was where the trust was. That's the basis of this relationship. I'd been rejected by the croc and I was leaving the next day. I wanted just one more chance to see if I could get some kind of peaceful response. Before I met Chito I would never consider engaging a 16-foot male croc on the surface.

"As the animal approached me what was constantly running through my mind was what Chito has taught me. The most critical thing is to be extremely confident because without doubt these animals can pick up on it if you are scared.

"As Pocho disengaged and swam past I reached out and

touched the dragon. Pocho seemed calm; not reacting to the touch but as he came around and circled me again I felt something had changed. He hit me and I felt really dreadful. You feel vulnerable with those teeth coming toward you. It's pretty scary but in my mind I really had a pleasant outcome."

"My relationship with this animal is very important for the entire world," Chito told the writer. "People don't understand but people like you who are close to nature can tell them the truth. This is why it is so important for you to be here because that way you can tell the world about my relationship and what it means for me as a human to have this friendship with Pocho."

"Chito's relationship with this ancient creature is based on over 20 years of commitment and love," wrote the writer. "The fact that humans have the potential to form deep bonds with a crocodile changes my whole belief in what I once thought of them as a cold, instinctive animal. I still have many questions but I leave behind perhaps the greatest mystery that I have ever seen with the knowledge that the primal connection I once felt with a croc in some caves in Africa was true. And that's where I thought this story ended. But a few months later I heard tragic news from Costa Rica that Pocho the croc had suddenly died of natural causes leaving Chito and family distraught. I wondered if the world would ever see a man and a croc in love again."

In his article for the *Tico Times* titled "Costa Rica says goodbye to famous croc Pocho" Matt Levin described the funeral for Poncho on October 17, 2011:

The final time Chito and Pocho took center stage seemed no less stirring, hard-to-believe and ridiculous than the act's original premise – a crocodile and a human as best friends.

After two decades of performing together, Pocho the "domesticated" crocodile died last Tuesday of natural causes in his manmade swamp at *Finca Las Tilapias*, in the Caribbean-slope town of Siquirres. The croc's owner, Gilberto Shedden, better

known as "Chito," said his partner was nearing 60 years old.

On Sunday – the day Pocho and Chito normally frolicked in the water for visitors – the village held a grand funeral for the huge reptile.

Chito placed the 5-meter, 450-kilo dead crocodile in a wagon and hitched it to a car that drove the duo around the town. Dozens of vehicles joined the motorcade. At least 50 mourners kept pace with the procession, while onlookers sprinted up to the cart to snap photos. By the time the tour ended, back at *Finca Las Tilapias*, some 300 people had shown up at the ranch.

"Our act was something very special," Chito, 54, said. "Always people who didn't know Pocho took something extraordinary from it."

Chito found Pocho wounded and near death on the shore of the Parismina River, in Limón province, in 1989. The crocodile had been shot in the left eye, and Chito nursed it back to health. A decade later, an employee at the *finca* saw Chito swimming with Pocho, and told local media. The unusual pair became stars after their first show in the summer of 2000. The ranch kept a veterinarian and a biologist to check on the crocodile's health. Pocho fed on 30 kilograms of fish and chicken a week.

Large crowds gathered weekly around the artificial lake to watch Pocho and Chito, with the crocodile performing tricks such as winking, rolling over and allowing Chito to put his head inside the giant's fang-lined mouth.

The memorial at *Finca Las Tilapias* recognized the croc's importance to the community. Onlookers watched Chito give a passionate goodbye to Pocho, the reptilian half of an act that became the biggest tourist attraction in the small, muggy pueblo and picked up coverage from around the world.

The funeral certainly seemed like the biggest event Siquirres had seen in some time. Chito's friends quoted Bible passages to the audience about loving animals. They dedicated songs to Pocho, and played videos of past performances and interviews with Chito.

"It was beautiful," Siquirres native Xinia Mejía, 40, said. "At least here, we've never seen anything like this."

Visitors from across the country came to observe the ceremony. Miguel Arias, 57, from San Carlos in northern Costa Rica, had never seen Chito and Pocho perform, but became interested after seeing a report on the news. Arias said he was stunned by the outpouring of support for the crocodile and the "beautiful" ceremony.

Funeral garb, however, was not required. Chito, dark-skinned, bald-headed and fit, dressed in the leopard-print loincloth and bandana he wore during his shows with Pocho. Many congregants wore T-shirts dedicated to Pocho's memory. The shirts sold for $4 at *Finca Las Tilapias*, alongside mugs dedicated to Chito and Pocho and a selection of small wooden crocodiles.

Pocho's carcass will be embalmed and placed on display at a museum at *Finca Las Tilapias.*

Skeptics may say the funeral was just a money-making charade, but Chito's copious tears did not appear to be of the crocodile variety. He seemed to need the attention and support of the crowd to stay composed. While other guests took the microphone to speak about Pocho, Chito could be seen bawling in the arms of his wife, Olga, or leaning over the crocodile with tears on his cheeks.

When Chito moved front and center again, he seemed determined to keep the last show with his "brother" Pocho as momentous as past ones. The most peculiar highlight – one that seemed to condense Chito's affection for Pocho and also his love for the limelight – came when he sang The Platters' classic "The Great Pretender." Chito wailed each lyric of the 1950s hit about denial to the fallen crocodile: "Oh yes I'm the great pretender / Pretending I'm doing well / My need is such I pretend too much / I'm lonely but no one can tell."

As Chito and Pocho's fame grew, there were those who suspected the croc would one day make "Chito *finito*" out of Shedden. Lolinda Mighty Hall, who grew up with Chito in Siquirres, remembered how fearful everyone was that the crocodile would turn on his trainer. Hall, 58, said over time they saw a genuine connection develop.

Other crocodiles later joined Pocho in Chito's swamp. The question circulated throughout the afternoon of whether Chito would soon begin training the next Pocho.

The speculation reached Chito midway through the ceremony. Replace Pocho? Chito sucked in a deep breath.

"Pocho is Pocho, the only one," Chito said, his voice cracking. "Much of the public and all the people of Siquirres agreed with him. There is no more Pocho. He will be the only Pocho there ever

was."

[Go to: THE MAN WHO SWIMS WITH CROCODILES on YouTube and you too can see Chito and his friend Pocho's awesome performance together.]

ABOUT THE AUTHOR

Author Robert F. Burgess grew up in Grand Rapids, Michigan. His books reflect his interest in adventuresome subjects ranging from scuba diving and sailing, to underwater archaeology and sport fishing. For more of his books please see his author's page on Amazon.com. The author now lives in northwest Florida. If you enjoyed reading this book please give it a star rating and tell others what you liked about it.

Other Books by Robert F. Burgess Available at Amazon.com

1. To Majorca With Love
2. Real Cliffhangers
3. Hemingway's Paris and Pamplona, Then and Now
4. Meeting Hemingway in Pamplona
5. Florida's Golden Galleons
6. Secret World Of The Sharks
7. Lone Wolf of the Wolfhounds
8. Secrets Of A Happy Hooker
9. Ghost Sniper
10. Return Of The Ghost Sniper
11. Revenge Of The Ghost Sniper
12. The Sweet Goodbye
13. Zapping The Zebra
14. Two For The Marquesas
15. Diving To Adventure
16. Sailing To Adventure
17. Find More Treasure
18. How They Escaped
19. Diving Into The Past
20. They Found Treasure
21. Fire, Ice And Inca Gold
22. Catch More Lobsters
23. Finding Sunken Treasure
24. 1715 Treasure
25. Tracking Treasure By Computer
26. One Night On Scarborough Pond
27. Sniper Up!
28. Charlie, You're Not Perfect
29. Rolling Thunder
30. Carlos Hathcock's Longest Mission
31. Mystery Snipers, CIA Wizardry, and Our Fight against Isis
32. Charlie Brown Sniper